LET'S REVEAL THE ECHOES OF LIFE

Whispers of our past & present for a loud future!

DEDICATION

This collection is dedicated to my grandfather, who always encouraged me to strive for excellence and instilled in me the love for writing. I am deeply grateful and thankful to him for shaping me into the person I have become.

And to the dreamers and the doers, the lost and the found. To those who have felt the sun's warmth and the night's cold embrace. To the seekers of truth and the lovers of beauty. To the resilient hearts that beat through trials and triumphs, and to the silent souls who find solace in the simple moments.

PREFACE

This book is a compilation of 50 pieces, each offering a diverse spectrum of motivational and self-realization reflections. These writings are crafted to bridge the gap between imagination and reality, with every piece uniquely unveiling the truths that often lie hidden in our minds. Each entry is rooted in the unspoken experiences of real life, and you may find that these insights resonate deeply, evoking a sense of personal connection and authenticity.

Great care has been taken to articulate thoughts, truths, and lessons in a way that is both accessible and impactful. The aim is to amplify these messages, sharing them with a broader audience for their enrichment and growth. This collection is more than just words on a page; it is a journey into the heart of human experience, designed to inspire, provoke thought, and ultimately, to foster a deeper understanding of ourselves and the world around us.

ACKNOWLEDGEMENTS

My deepest gratitude goes out to all the people and experiences around me, which have been a wellspring of inspiration and content for this book. Every moment, every encounter, and every situation contributed to shaping these writings.

I want to express my heartfelt thanks to my parents, family, and friends. Their support has been the cornerstone of this journey. They not only motivated me but also provided the strength and reassurance needed to see this project through.

I would also like to extend my sincere thanks to Craiyon, a free AI image generator, for its invaluable assistance in creating the stunning visuals featured in this book.

CONTENTS

Oo MOM YOU ARE....

My sleep at 6 in the morning is due,
You are already ready with my day's schedule.
My younger sibling is still in his dreams,
My mother is worried about today's test it seems.
Mother, you have so many things to remember and
jot down,
If anything goes haywire, we are the first ones to
frown.
Oh, Mom you are an eternal burning candle,
Darkness from life you disappear and how
effortlessly things you handle.

Dad wants everything on time,
Mom controls his anger just by mime.
She is a woman of million hands,
Beside her anyone cannot stand.
The food she cooks is palatable,
The aroma itself makes us unstable.
Oh, Mom your hand knows magic,
You can even heal a person's tragic.

Her tears roll down upon her cheeks,
If her family in turmoil she sees.
Those pearls can never be returned.
Before it diamond is also churned.
Her smile hides all her pain.
I wish her life never goes in vain.
Oh, Mom you are perfect among humans.

Before you, scared are the demons.

Her beauty and style are haute couture,
We have to forget the pain, to reach her stature.
Mom brought me out of her womb,
Even though I was a girl, she never thought of a tomb.
Taught me to fight with the world so nefarious,
Towards her aim she is always serious.
Oh, Mom you are my mentor,
Tell me, how service to you I render?

YOU WON'T UNDERSTAND BEFORE TIME!

Sitting on my school bench one fine day, I pondered the possibilities that awaited me in adulthood.

The prospect of making my own decisions and navigating the world independently filled me with excitement.

No longer would I be bound by the constraints of parental approval or societal expectations.

Instead, I envisioned a future where I worked for a prestigious multinational corporation, earning my own money and having the freedom to spend it as I pleased.

The idea of financial independence exhilarated me – no longer relying on others for my needs or desires.

Fear would hold no power over me, I would confidently assert my beliefs and convictions.

The world would become my playground, ripe for exploration and discovery without the need for permission.

I anticipated forming new connections, expanding my social circle, and ultimately achieving success that would inspire others to follow in my footsteps.

As I indulged in these thoughts, my eyes shimmered with the brilliance of my dreams, igniting a sense of anticipation and possibility within me.

However, reality proved to be vastly different and more challenging than I had anticipated.

Some life decisions weighed so heavily on me that I found myself paralyzed with fear, unable to make them without seeking counsel from others.

There were moments when I longed for the familiar comfort of my parents' guidance and approval, yearning to feel like their little kid again rather than a grown-up facing the harsh realities of the world.

The corporate world, far from the glamorous image I had imagined, came with its own share of trials: stress, pressure, office politics, and an imbalance between work and personal life.

Despite having my own financial resources now, I found myself lacking the time and freedom to enjoy them or explore the world as I had once dreamed.

My health and lifestyle demanded attention, yet I found myself alone in managing these responsibilities.

Expanding my social circle brought not only new connections but also the weight of judgment, peer pressure, and the need for validation, leaving me feeling increasingly detached from my authentic self.

Even in my success, I found the insatiable hunger for greater achievements still lingering, leaving me perpetually unsatisfied.

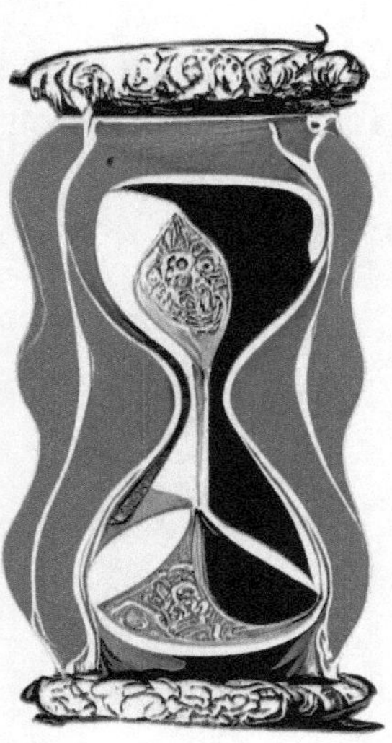

BURNOUT TO RECOVERY

I considered myself strong enough to deal with anything,
But the weaknesses inside me were trying to speak something.
I knew I can make anything possible with my willingness and belief,
I was in this world tree, a never falling leaf.

I refused to believe that I needed peace too,
I refused to believe that I would ruin my health too.
For me, my ambitions took priority over all the stuff,
Not realising that handling heath and sanity would become tough.

Thinking my body can take a back seat till I become successful,
Instead of creating a balance, a mistake too awful.
I started loosing focus and my targets became blurry,
I was still immersed in an illusion blanket, so furry.

I didn't understand why people empathised a lot on
mental health,
I didn't understand why it was okay to deprioritise
wealth.
I didn't care about my lifestyle and eating habits,
I was unaware about all the problems my body
inhabits.

When my body reached a tolerance saturation,
And my mind was filled with stress and confusion,
Reality hit me hard and I became clueless,
Not able to control the anxiety, feeling my life is
useless.

I pushed myself and tried to cope with the world,
But it hit me back and again I was hurled.
I became helpless and left all that I yearned,
It became difficult to live the life I earned.

My health and lifestyle became my priority,
With confidence, love and happiness paucity,
I set myself free from all the anxiety and negative
vibes melt,
To regain my mental, spiritual, physical and
emotional health.

I can certainly feel the difference now,
Good health and positive vibes is what I allow.
I believe I was missing on the most significant
routine,

Start with health, family, love, happiness and everything else in between.

LIFE'S JOURNEY

Stage 1 of life begins with **Prenatal Development,**
That's the time for the new life's
acknowledgement.
With lots of complications and intensive care;
For a mother, this phase is certainly a nightmare.

Infancy and Toddlerhood stage comes next,
All about transformation and reflex.
Dynamic growth and brain development are
this stage traits,
Giving lifetime memories and interesting tales.

Stage 3 is reserved for **Childhood,**
Exploring all sorts of activities that one should.
Beginning to learn the workings of the
physical world,
With greater sense of self by being ruffled.

Said to be the most important stage,
Between child and adult is its range.
Increased decision making and search for self;
Adolescence influences one to be a conformist
or a rebel.

Stage 5 is the attainment of full physical
and intellectual maturity,
With lots of privileges and pressure about
family security.
It is characterised by full stability
and responsibility of oneself,
Adulthood as a word is being independent
in itself.

Stage 6 is what we call as the **Old Age,**
Considered as life's last page.
Healthcare, psychological and emotional needs
are a concern,
Peace and connect with supreme power is
what this stage will yearn.

EMRACE SELF WORTH & INDIVIDUALITY

Every single step I take matters a lot;
Whether it is astray or appropriate people sort.

My intentions the world might not get,
Even if, through my deeds, all their expectations
are met.

Whenever I think of doing and starting something
new,
I start ruminating on what would be the world's
review.

Will this step give them an opportunity of evil
talk?
Will it be the correct path for me to easily walk?

Why does their inference affect me?
Why all the aspects through their eyes I see?

In this free world why am I not emancipated?
Why do I get by the world rated?

Why my life is not my own?
Why does the world rejoice when I am torn?

I am too afraid of the hearsay;
For "Black sheep of the family" they may say.

When I did well I heard it never,
When I did wrong I heard it ever.

The bud within me is trying to blossom,
Because of the evil communications I should not
let it rotten!

EARN FOR YOUR LIVING

Orders are out, government employees are transferred,
To this verdict they have surrendered.
Leave no stone unturned for shilling without cribbing,
Society says "Earn for your own living".

The crop season has ceased.
Farmers to their owners have pleased.
"Give some work, make us employed",
"What is the reason? Are you annoyed?"
"The season is over so stop pitching".
Owner says, "Now earn for your own living".

The teacher is working hard for the future of her students,
Even if her pupils are impudent.
The flowers of tomorrow and the seeds of today are in teacher's hand.
She has a great role and responsibility to play to help them out-stand.
Rebuked for scolding a student for the indiscipline.
Even if it was to make the pupil a good citizen.
The principal calls the teacher's behaviour unforgiving.
The principal says, "Now earn for your own living".

Critics become actors achilles heel,
Actors career's some part depends on the critics
seal.
Media behind them is always on the run,
After a box office flop they are regarded as no one.
And when their no film is releasing,
Industry says, "Now earn for your own living".

There is another set of people who govern the
country.
Their actions are watched by each and every.
The clamour and peace depends on their decisions,
Among themselves they have a lot of frictions.
Losing votes is quite ailing.
People say, "Now earn for your own living".

This is not the end of the day.
The sun's ray might not be yours today.
There are various such examples and laws of
living,
Decide whether they are healing or tormenting.

RISE & SHINE

When you see hindrances & obstacles your way, you may SLOW DOWN but don't STOP!

When you have to put your point across, be ASSERTIVE but never RUDE!

When you are uncertain about any situation or future event, don't try to think over it and suffer in IMAGINATION more than what REALITY has to offer.

When you see a need to prove yourself to anyone, don't TWINE yourself in the game, simply WALK AWAY!

When you feel that you have GONE THROUGH & SUFFERED a lot, remember you have INTERESTING STORIES & EXPERIENCES to share later.

When you are at the crossroads, don't STEP BACK, choose your path and walk over it with PRIDE!

When the world rushes, you don't have to RUSH with them, always be at your own PACE!

When you see others doing well in life, don't be
JEALOUS, be MOTIVATED!

REMEMBER AND UNDERSTAND WHERE TO
MAKE SILENCE SILVER & SPEECH GOLD
OR VICE VERSA!

CONTENTMENT

Have you ever felt low without a reason?
Even if there are countless reasons to be content?
Have you ever wondered why this could be?
Have you ever tried to keep a check on stress?

The world is running and so are we trying to
catchup.
Increase in stress and expectation levels supersedes
our ability to relax.
We often forget that life is unpredictable.
It can be at times brutal and at times blessed but
the stretch is uncertain.
We often try to control what's not in our hands and
in the interim lose on the controllable aspects.

When our planning fails life gets another chance to
learn & grow.
We are often least bothered about the journey.
Our vision is fixed at what the destination has to
offer.
And when destination turns out to be a disaster we
overlook the journey, no matter how enthralling it
might be.

Contentment seems like impossible to achieve for
human race.
We are in unceasing search of something or the
other.

We are not moving but rushing in our lives,
Giving a way for an incessant feeling of gloom.

Though we come a long way in our life, our hearts
remain hollow.
The void instead of getting filled widens up due to
discontent.
Stop, breathe and celebrate the trivial moments.
Be proud of yourself for making it this far because
it's your life and you are its master.

DELULU

Thinking of "Overthinking" and then
"Overthinking",
 Expecting to get "Expectations" met by
"Expecting" from others,
"Blaming" oneself for "Blaming" others and then
again playing the "Blame" game,
Talking of "Work life Balance" and then creating
"Imbalance" ourselves,
"Proving" ourselves that we are not "Proving" our
worth to the world but still try   "Proving" the
world,
"Successful" yet measuring "Success" with the
"Success" parameters set by others,
Talking of small "Steps" at a time yet "Stepping"
onto big leaps,
Trying to "Control" "Controls" beyond our
"Control",
Taking away the "Present" of "Present" and
"Presenting" our mind with the past and the
future,

The lines sound simple yet are so deep! Read
Again!

EXISTENTIAL CRISIS

Holding onto people and emotions will eventually saturate us.

Saturate us to the extent that we won't be able to recognize our own worth.

Our worth will be taken for granted not only by others but also by our own selves.

Self-love will gradually vanish which will lead to existential crises.

Existential crises to the extent that we will start questioning our life's existence.

Our life will no longer be our own and our towpath will be in the hands of others.

The towpath will be pulled by the world to suit their needs and wants.

Their needs and wants will be fulfilled to the extent that we will start forgetting the purpose of our own living.

Nothing will be left with us which we would be able to call our own.

We would be twined in a web created by holding onto our emotions.

Holding onto emotions to the extent that we will have a lot of inlets and zero outlets.

And by the time we will sense the malfeasance, we would be the victims of our own designs.

The power of releasing irrespective of any parameter should be instilled and ignited from within.

This power will help us to the extent that nobody but we would be the master of our life and would change Existential Crisis to Self-Reliance.

EXPLORING LEADERSHIP ARCHETYPES

"BOSS"- Quite a heavy word, right?
Who is he/she exactly? What is his/her exact role?
The one who supervises us or the one who lays down
the authority?

Authority? Then who is a DICTATOR? How to we
define a Dictator?
The one who gets his/her job done at the cost of others?
The one who thinks oneself supreme? Or the one who
leads others?

Leads? Then who is a LEADER? What is a leader's
part?
To be upfront and carry others along? To be a backbone
of others? To rally people to move forward? To see a
vision for the entire unit? To knit and manage all?

Manage all? Then who is a MANAGER? How is he/
she placed?
A person responsible for controlling a group? A person
responsible for administering? A person who can
manage and allocate the resources well?

Well, a BOSS, a DICTATOR, a LEADER & a
MANAGER can be the same with a pinch of every
character, situational or absolute, or can be altogether
different.

Just to demarcate; A BOSS acts as the literal head, A
DICTATOR acts as the
oppressor, A LEADER a mentor & A MANGER is an
operator.

DECIDE WHO YOU ARE AND WHO YOU WANT
TO BE!

THE EVOLUTION

Time is flowing! It always did. With time everything is changing. Changes always took place. Then what's new now?

THE RAPIDITY OF THE CHANGE WITH TIME IS NEW!

From stone & metal, to clay tablets, to papyrus, to animal skin, to birch bark, to palm leaf and to paper is how our writing materials evolved. But did it stop here? No, it again evolved and now we also write or type on tablets/ laptops/desktops.

From using plants as clothes, to using animal skin, to weaving and spinning plant and animal fibers, to using manmade and synthetic fibers, is how our clothing evolved.

From using branches and saplings, to building huts with thick logs, to using stones, to building shelters with various kinds of other synthetic materials, is how our shelters evolved.

From eating plants, to eating raw animals, to learning to heat and cook on fire, to adding flavors and enhancing it according to our taste buds, is how our food evolved.

From smoke signals, to making sounds, to using gestures, to using words, to messenger pigeons, to telephones and emails, to video calls, is how our communication evolved.

From walking long distances, to travelling on animals, to inventing wheels, to using land and water ways for travelling, to using air ways, is how our transportation evolved.

Anything and everything has evolved. Of course, it is for a better good, bringing along its set of cons. And of course, the way education is imparted, to how the country runs, to how people do official work, to how people have different lifestyle opinions, to how people find their soulmates, all of this has switched.

But do you know what has not changed?

THE LOAD OF OUR PAST AND THE PRESUMPTIONS OF OUR FUTURE, which lingers inside us and we hide ourselves in its periphery.

KEY PRINCIPLES & LAWS

"Work smarter, not harder," aligns with the 80-20
principle,
Suggesting that 80% of the results come from 20%
of the effort. Is this really possible?
Absolutely. It requires brainstorming and
prioritization,
Along with an understanding of return and
effective presentation.

"Work expands to fill the time allotted for its
completion";
This is the Parkinson's law which explains work's
accretion.
The law is important to make realistic deadlines;
To save oneself from red lines.

"90% of everything is crap".
Be vigilant enough to find this gap.
This is the Sturgeon's law, which talks about
finding the rice grains from the chaff.
Even if much intricate is the graph.

"The rich get richer; the poor get poorer".
This adage is not a kind of rumor,
As this is applicable to fame, status and economic
capital,
To solve this is the need of the hour, before it
reaches its apical.

"1% of the people create content, 9% change or update content whereas 99% of the people consume content".
Most of us like to consume without effort, this is what it meant.
This is the 1% rule or the 90-9-1 rule of the internet culture;
Dealing with the creators, contributors and lurkers percentage structure.

We also have the theory of human motivation,
Which has the psychological relation.
This is Maslow's principle of the hierarchy of needs,
Starting from the bottom psychological needs to self-actualization, this theory leads.

Well, whatever be the law, principle or theory,
Remember, not to interpret in the way which is eerie.

GUILT: HINDRANCE OR CATALYST

Compromising on our own standards of conduct
provides a path for guilt to creep in,
Making us entangled and suffocated under the
burden of the sin.
Paying the price for the violation and mess,
Is like a notice of an uninvited cess.

Guilt can be normal when feelings interfere with
our life,
Finding an outlet becomes tough as they become
rife.
A self-conscious emotion, if controlled and
rectified,
Can work towards betterment if testified.

A feeling of guilt takes birth quite early and with
time its intensity increases.
When we actually acknowledge, it gets
overpowered by our caprices.
Overthinking can raise a non-genuine guilt,
Which can make a beautiful life filth.

Hence, a guilt can have two roles to play in our life,
It can either hold us back or can provide a new perspective to strive.
Choosing either of the two is always an individual's option,
Self-introspection will help us in its adoption.

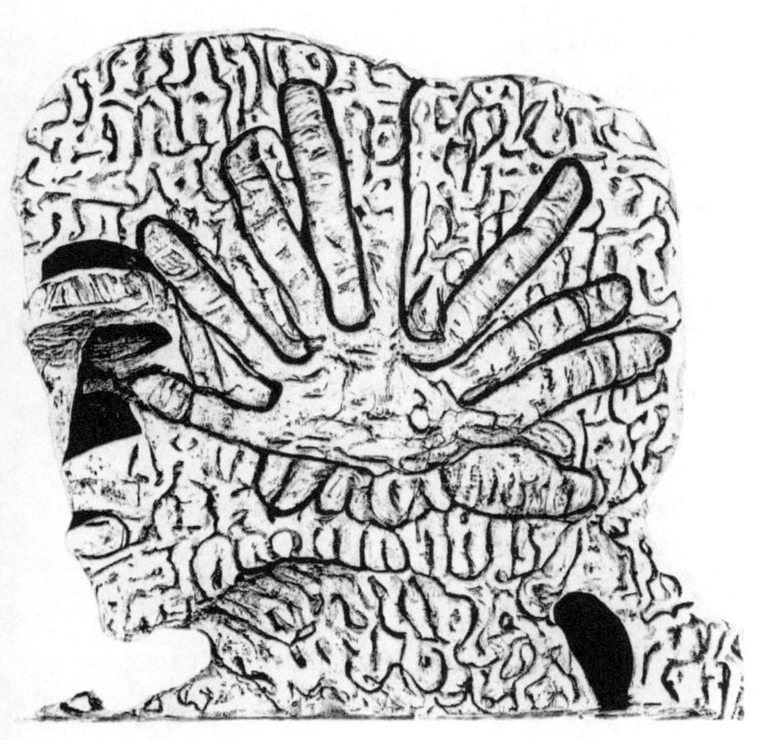

A DREAMY CITY

I went into a city of paradise.
Believe me, my experience was not nice.

No ditch, no trench and no pebble;
It was nearly unacceptable for a rebel.

The whole system was not at all slovenly,
To my astonishment I heard a grass speak
suddenly.

"Hello! My name is Miss Grace.
Kindly turn around and show me your face"

I asked, "Which place is this?"
It requested, "Kindly close your fist."

Miss Grace touched my hand gently.
And whispered some words quietly.

I opened my fist to see the name of the place.
"All's well" was the name of the paradise space.

The grass asked me to sit for the whole story.
I wasn't interested in its glory.

I walked through a narrow passage;
A giant rock was waiting to take my advantage.

The rock could walk and talk.
And had large round eyes to stalk.

I wished it to be a dream.
Went ahead to see a stream.

The stream was red in colour.
Seemed to be full of valour.

Was flowing quietly with no noise.
Surprisingly spoke to me in a harsh voice.

"I am carrying the blood of selfish human;
To you I would like to summon"

"Tell me why humans are so greedy,
And turn a blind eye to the needy"

I was filled with shame.
Now I wanted no fame.

I went ahead with my trembling feet;
To find someone like me, whom I could meet.

"I will cover the whole world under me;
And will leisurely enjoy a cup of tea."

I took a long sigh,
And looked up towards the sky.

I asked, "Why are you doing so?
Are we humans your foe?"

"You find the answer to it yourself,
Go to flashback to see how we felt"

I got up from this dreamy city nightmare;
That very morning I was filled with despair.

SEVEN MYSTERIES

Many mysteries, many unsolved,
Though many generations have evolved.

Is there anyone who can let the cat out of the bag?
And remove from a story the mystery tag?

To mention and name all mysteries is quite
daunting.
We'll certainly run short of counting.

So let's unfold a few;
With some let's cut & sew.

The floral designs appearing all over mysteriously
centuries ago,
Known as the crop circles, ignoring it some said,
"let it go".

The masonry pyramid structures located in Egypt;
Eased the monarchs afterlife passage, says the
script.

Now let's talk about the Bigfoot aka Sasquatch.
With humans it has found a perfect match.

The Belmez Faces being the fourth.
They mysteriously appeared and disappeared from
walls and floor.

Next in my list is the Stone Henge.
Putting them in place needs great strength.

Bermuda Triangle in my list comes on the sixth
place,
Its story of disappearing objects is perfect one for a
scare.

Last and the seventh on my list is the mystery of
Anastasia; daughter of Nicholas II,
Who survived in the Russian revolution yet her
existence is without any clue.

The seven mysteries now come to an end.
There are many more to find & mend.

RETRIBUTION

"Forgive and forget" reminds me of the value of forgiveness I learned in my moral science classes.

Toughest value to follow and abide by because a feeling of retribution always finds a loophole.

Retribution not only creates clamour in the life of someone ought to receive it but makes the giver deranged too.

"If someone is at their worse, be at your best" is heard quite often.

Even if we are hurt awfully by the person who has an excuse of going through rough times.

Easier said than done right? Only the one who goes through knows the real feeling of leaving behind and moving ahead.

Then why should we avoid retribution?

There is only one moral justification for it - The guilty will get what they deserve, the innocent will feel safe and secure, the society will recover and the faith and trust will blossom.

Other than this, retribution is seen as something distressing.

To put it in simple words, "An eye for an eye, makes the whole world blind" - Mahatma Gandhi's words can be compared with the retribution consequences.

It is very important to learn to segregate and differentiate what calls for retribution and what should be forgiven and forgotten.

Unnecessary regression just to maintain stature is of no use as it not only will be rough on the opposite party but will also have major consequences on the one practising it.

Though Miles Franklin always said, "There is a law of retribution in all things, direct or indirect, visible or invisible" but that law should only come into effect if the offender realises why retribution has come upon him

Because as per version of Arthur Doyle, there is no satisfaction in vengeance unless the offender knows and realises the reason!

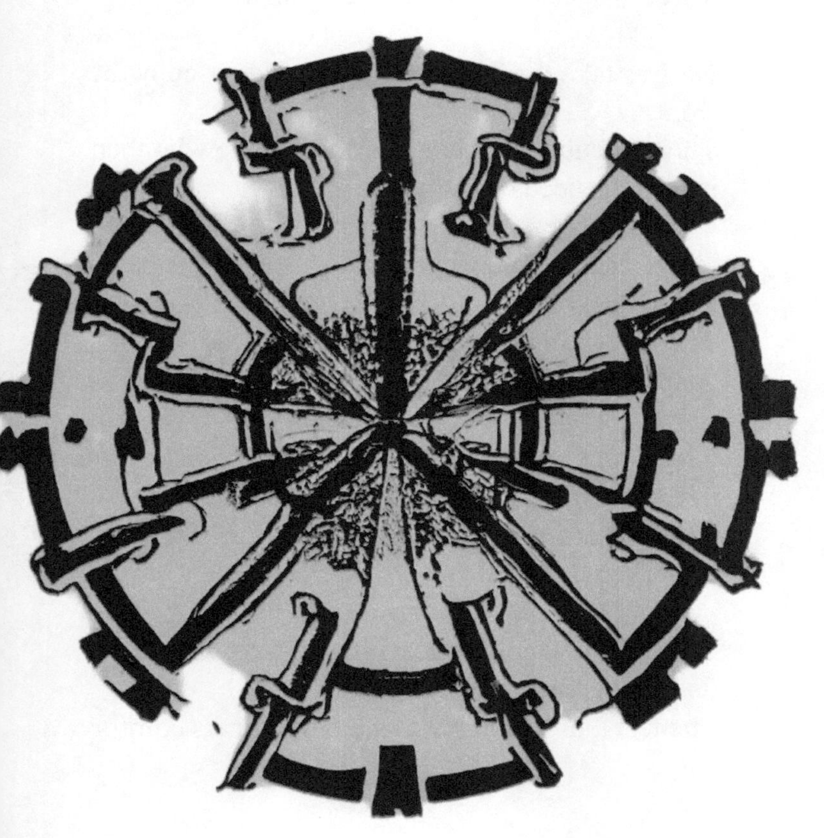

CROSSROADS

When everything seems sorted and as per plan,
There is a sudden shift, in the blink of an eye.

Desires take the back seat to let needs occupy the
front.
The contentment is retained for the one who then
makes his needs turn into desires.

Crossroads hold no significance then as the path is
already chosen,
The fire within is either dormant or dead and
adaptation mode is active.

Crossroads are for the ones who do not make their
needs, their desires as per situation.
Crossroads test how strongly one wants ones
desires to be fulfilled.

The test on which far reaching consequences
depend,
The test that would push one out of one's comfort
zone,

The test that would require self perusal,
The test that would require a strong will.

The fear of losing, pulls one back and the will to
pull through makes one victorious.

Even though the historic footprints may not be present to guide one, the resolution to conquer the desires will play the guide.

The one who knows how to quantify the importance to be given to whatever one wishes to have or do in life can smoothly sail through the austerities of life.
And in the interim one might lose the battle to eventually win the war.

COLOURS DUAL NATURE

Red is the most passionate colour, symbolising
love, courage and *religious fervour*.
Red is a sign of *danger and anger hence* its
thought gives *tremor*.

Blue represents *inspiration, freedom &
imagination*.
Greek mythology associates it with *rain, sadness
and dissatisfaction*.

Green is a nature dominant colour symbolising
new beginnings and renewal.
Excess of green brings in *stagnation & boredom*
and people might seek for its removal.

Orange is as *joyous, enthusiastic & balanced* as
can be.
The warmth veil can *deceive* and can turn out to be
unworthy.

The colour White radiates *innocence & purity*.
It also makes one feel *cold, isolated & empty*.

Black reflects comfort, *protection &
sophistication*.
It can also be a sign of *aloofness & depression*.

Yellow being the most *vibrant* colour of the lot.
It is also associated with the *sickness rot.*

Silver is a colour of *grace, sheen & elegance.*
It can also be misunderstood as *coldness &
arrogance.*

Solid colour Brown is *resilient & dependable.*
It can also make one feel *heavy & dull.*

The colour Grey is as *neutral & modest* as can be.
It reflects *old age, indifference & uncertainty.*

Pink is the most tender colour symbolising
romance.
It is also a sign of taking life decisions *perchance.*

Gold being the most precious colour depicting
wealth & prosperity.
It can also be misunderstood as a colour *lacking
kindness & generosity.*

There are countless colours to make us feel lucid.
No wonder, they can also turn out to be lurid.

The worth of joy & happiness is realised,
Only when sorrow in life is equalised.

HUMAN CONNECTIONS TRANSFORMATIVE POWER

The face that rekindles hope,
The incomplete love that feels complete,
The smile that tells us to count our blessings,
The gratitude that unlocks the fullness of life,
The humility that we often forget,
The compassion that makes us human,
The work that is appreciated,
The touch that heals the wound,
The immaculate thoughts that purify the air,
The eyes that persuade frequent arrival,
The need that becomes a desire,
The stranger who becomes an acquaintance,
The abandoned who feels cherished!

CLASSROOM TO CORPORATE

The road from classroom to corporate is certainly
not an easy one.
While classrooms provide valuable knowledge,
corporate gives important life lesson.

With financial literacy becoming the need of the
hour for stability and success,
It is crucial for classrooms to provide all the right
financial mentoring access.

Emotional intelligence holds greater significance
than intellectual intelligence
As it encompasses the ability to manage emotions
and navigate social interactions without any fence.

In the classroom, intellectual intelligence (IQ)
tends to be prioritised over emotional intelligence
(EQ), despite the latter's significance in personal
and professional development.
EQ's influence on how individuals handle stress,
resolve conflicts, and make decisions is quite
prevalent.

Critical thinking and problem-solving skills are
typically acquired beyond the confines of the
classroom, as the scenarios necessitating their
application often lie outside the scope of
traditional curriculum.

These certain skills are often overlooked but are crucial for navigating real life situations and hence classrooms should be more meticulous.

Throughout our lives, we frequently encounter challenging decision-making situations.
Learning how to make informed decisions, weigh options and consider consequences is vital for navigating life's variations.

In classrooms, we often feel sheltered and insulated, focusing solely on our studies without much regard for the realities of the world beyond.
When faced with real-life situations, we often find ourselves unprepared and unsure of how to respond.

In the age of digitalisation and widespread access to online information, it is crucial to integrate digital literacy into classroom education,
To ensure classrooms' ability to apply knowledge to real-world contexts and to also know the right consumption and interpretation.

GENDER ROLES

Great muscle and body mass,
Is said to be the characteristic of a lad.
Soft and gentle body texture,
Is typically possessed by a lass.

With different reproductive systems and
anatomical characteristics,
Behavioural development becomes an important
parameter for hormonal statistics.
Women have accumulated tissue around hips and
thighs,
As opposed to the accumulation in men around
abdomen and trunk highs.

Men have 10% larger brains they say,
Though women's memorization and learning
power is better as per survey.
Men are tilted towards the left side of the brain,
While women have a more balanced terrain.

Oestrogen and Progesterone are lass's priced
hormones,
While lad's primary one is Testosterone hormone.
Women face fluctuations in hormones more in
number
Whether it is autumn, winter, spring or summer.

Strength, aggression and dominance are associated
with masculinity,
Passivity, nurturing and subordination usually with
feminity.
But these have become a thing of the past,
Roles are shared and intertwined as gender
segregation doesn't last.

Socially women are more aligned towards
compassion, politeness and enthusiasm,
Men scoring higher on intellect, assertiveness and
industriousness idiasm.
An extrovert and outgoing female is not liked by
all,
An introvert and reserved male is said to face a
downfall.

Females develop language skills and have better
vocabulary,
While males are good with logical and mental
ability.
Cultural beliefs, traditions, and societal norms
contribute more to differences,
Males and females are subject to set standard
societal preferences.

Evolutionary perspectives state that women have
higher parental investment,
Carrying the child during pregnancy and producing
food for the infant becomes its testament.

The roles are attributed to the historic hunter-
gatherer society,
Which paved way for psychologists to come to
such propriety.
Whatever be the established notions and taboos,
Men and women can now do anything in all views.
What is important is the work, determination and
patience,
That can provide freedom and make one
complacent.

LET'S TURN TO THE STARS

Astrological sun signs are based on position of the
sun at the time of the birth they say,
Determining personality, compatibility, connection
to the universe and ones social way.

Energetic, bold, ambitious and competitive is the
sun sign Aries,
Their enthusiasm and impulsiveness is greater than
the ferries.

Reliable, patient, practical and determined are the
Taureans,
Loyal, grounded, humble but stubborn, says the
editorials.

Gemini, the air sign is adaptable, outgoing and
intelligent,
Known for versatility, quick wit but sometimes
inconsistent.

Emotional, nurturing, intuitive are the Cancerians
with empathetic heart,
Protective, sensitive, moody with overly cautious
start.

The fire sign Leo is charismatic, generous and
confident.
Are good performers but can also be arrogant and
self centered.

Virgos are analytical, meticulous, reliable and
hardworking,
Organized, helpful, but overly critical and
perfectionistic.

Diplomatic, charming and fair minded are the
Libras,
Social, cooperative, good at mediating conflicts
but are people pleasers.

Scorpions are intense, resourceful, determined and
perceptive,
They are fiercely loyal, brave but can be secretive
and possessive.

Adventurous, optimistic and independent are the
Sagittarius,
Open minded, exploratory but are sometimes
reckless and create fuss.

Capricorns are said to be ambitious, responsible
and disciplined,
Goal oriented, persistent but sometimes overly
serious and reserved.

Aquarians are known to be innovative,
humanitarian and intellectual,
Original, idealistic but can sometimes be aloof and
unpredictable.

Compassionate, artistic, creative and highly
imaginative are Pisceans,
Intuitive, empathetic but are sometimes escapist
and overly sensitive during crisis.

LIFE'S MOMENTS INTERCONNECTEDNESS

Life is a journey filled with numerous challenges,
obstacles, and problems,
Acknowledging and dealing with these is certainly
essential.
Learnings from mistakes committed during such times
teach important life lessons,
And make one resilient, stronger and a fearless person.

Life is a journey filled with numerous changes,
transformations and transitions,
Adapting to these fosters flexibility, contentment, and
situation admissions.
Transitions play a significant role in coming out of
comfort zone and hence should be marked,
As they serve as the starting point of the successful
journeys embarked.

Milestones give us a feeling of celebration and
commemoration,
And a confidence in handling all pits, transitions and in
building connections.
No moment is insignificant as all are connected and
twined,
As after every downfall there is growth and success
defined.

Hence, it is important to live every moment,
Even if the circumstance is not cogent,
Everything happens for a reason
And every joy has its own season.

ELDERLY COMPASSION

The wrinkles personified the experience and time,
In some scenarios they could only mime,

Their smile hid the underneath pain and suffering,
Few were unsure of their old age home stay
reasoning.

All had different experiences to share and family
stories to tell,
Though in the shelter home they belonged to the
same personnel.

Few still missed their children and grand children,
While few became ignorant and were still on the
internal run.

The withered teeth and grey hair signified age
milestone,
Aged dealt with diminishing sensory functions and
mobility with no moan.

Few were just counting their days,
While others were enjoying in their own ways.

Old age, said to be the most difficult time of life,
It is hard during this to keep everything fine.

A world where everyone states that they are busy,
Increase in old age homes is a sight not at all
pretty.

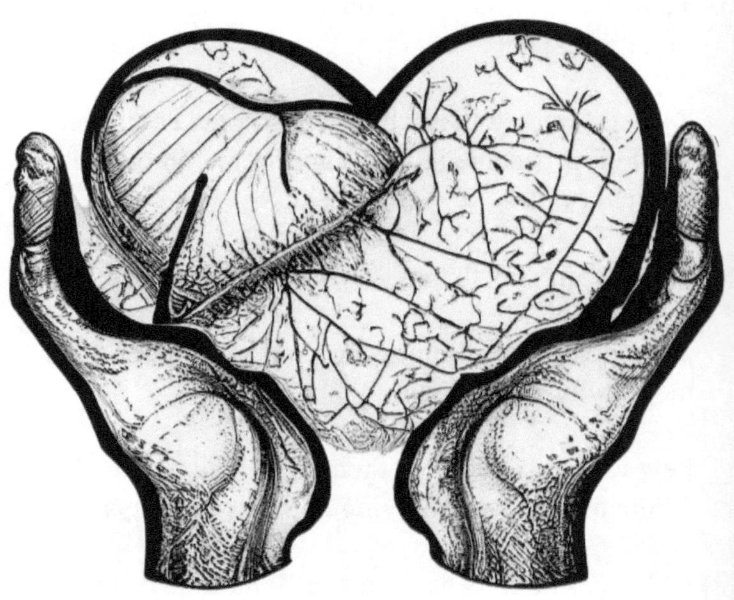

SCAMS

Does experiencing a scam make someone feel
foolish and unintelligent, or does it serve as a
valuable lesson to exercise caution in the future?
The response to this situation only depends on the
individual who has directly experienced being
scammed irrespective of the stature.

Fraudulent emails, messages, or websites that
mimic legitimate ones to trick people fall under
Phishing scams,
Those promising high returns with little or no risk
or Ponzi and pyramid schemes are a part of
Investment scams.

Tech support scams involve scammers posing as
tech support agents, claiming there's a problem
with ones computer or device,
Romance scams involves building relationship and
extorting money through dating websites.

In Lottery scams, victims are informed that they've
won a lottery, but need to pay a fee to claim it.
Though in reality, there's no prize, and the
scammers disappear with the money.
Fake charities exploit people's generosity and
shrink the chances when the actual need arises for
legitimate charity

Stealing someone's personal information, social
security and credit card details are a part of
Identity theft,
Promising easy money for little work and leading
one into illegal activities is a part of work from
home arrest.

Binary options trading platforms manipulate or
misrepresent information to deceive investors into
believing they can profit from trading options,
Tricking renters into paying deposits or rent
upfront for illegal /disowned properties is heinous
rental scam adoptions.

Scams are not easy to identify and to deal with,
Falling into the scam trap is certainly not a myth.

All one needs is alertness and awareness against
getting scammed,
Even if the scam strategy is difficult to interpret
and understand.

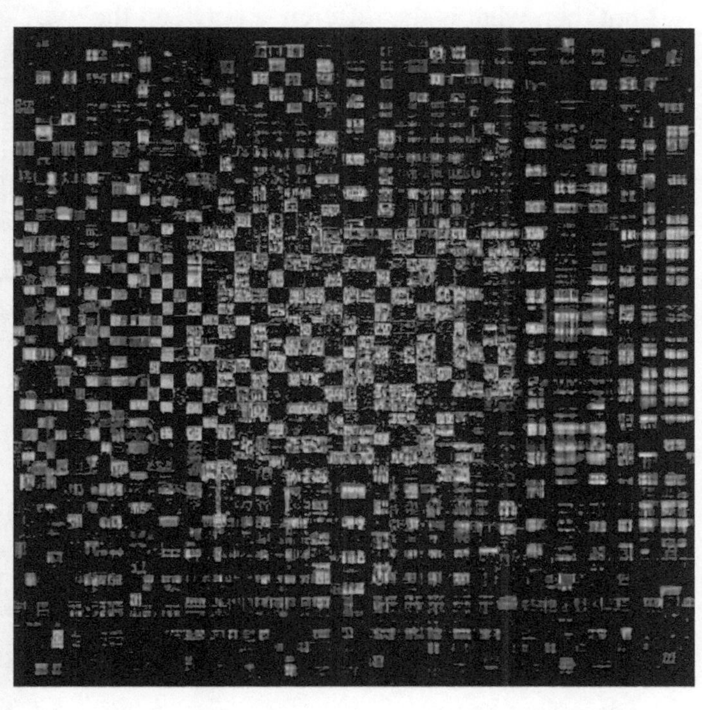

STRIKE A BALANCE

Does being an orthodox or being a conservative
same?
If not then what is the difference between the two?
Is it good to be either of the two?
If not these two, then what else one should be?

Firstly, orthodoxy is following beliefs (especially
religious), staunchly,
It can accommodate any amendments or additions
as long as they are related to religious views.

Conservatism on the other hand is being averse to
any change to ones beliefs or established rules and
principles. They need not be religious in particular.
Conservatives act in contrast to liberalism and the
orthodox can never compromise their faith.

Being any one of them is acceptable up to a certain
limit but if one of them exceeds, it can cause great
havoc not only to ones life but also to the lives of
the associated ones.
So, add a flavour of progressiveness, to have a
gamut of flavours and savour the right ones at the
right time!

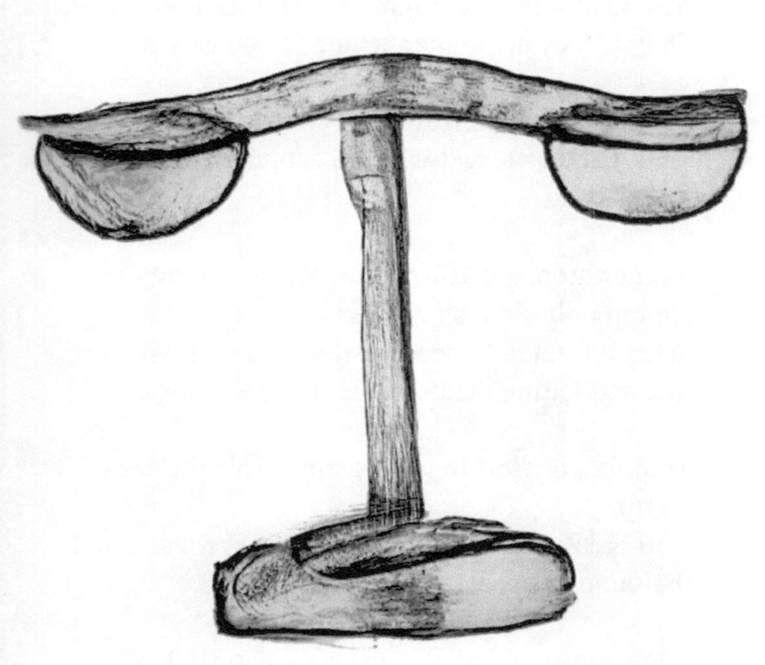

SELF ACCEPTANCE

In our lives, we tend to seek a lot of validations.
We come across people who may not provide us
genuine feedbacks.

Yes, feedbacks are important for ones upliftment,
Only if they are authentic and are constructive.

Seeking validations for everything we do in life,
Will make us forget who we actually are and what
is our stand.

Recognition and affirmation for the validity is
elating only for a short span of time.
What we actually need is silently doing what we
like and letting the outcome make the noise.

Trapping oneself in getting approvals for ones
worth,
Will break one from within if the approval is not
the same as expected.

The day we realize that the only permission or
validation that matters is our own,
We would start living our life in the true sense with
zero expectations.

Because if we are surviving on compliments,
We'll ultimately be crushed by criticisms.

DEAD HABITS

For some, dead habits are mindless whereas for
others these influence decisions.
Dead habits block the inflow of progressive
thoughts & ideas.

They are followed all over the world with slight
variations,
And can cause obscurity when followed blindly.

Mostly these habits are imposed on the newer
generations by the older.
Eventually these get carried on with generations
unless someone turns a rebel.

Some people practise these for the sake of
receiving success,
While others practise for the sake of satisfaction.

"Beginners luck" is what saves the master from the
disgrace.
Even though the newbie has set up a strong base.

Found a penny? Pick it up! The good luck is yours;
Who knows whether good luck or bad luck a
person endures.

Walking under a ladder is said to be blasphemous,
Though the reason of stumbling someone should
be unanimous.

Black cats crossing your path is a curse!
Then people with pet cats should be at their worse?

"Bad luck comes in threes"
Waiting for a consecutive bad luck will certainly
attract three.

"Breaking a mirror is synonymous to seven years
of bad luck"
They say inside a mirror our soul pieces are stuck.

"666" is said to be a number of the beast,
Numbers also have an inside story feast?

"Knock on the wood" is the most widely heard
dead habit,
They say good spirit is what trees/wood inhabit.

From crossing fingers literally to just saying
"fingers crossed";
Can sooth us and make the hard times' mental
impact soft.

Don't open umbrella indoors, not because it would poke someone's eye,
But because it can bring misfortune and bad luck tide.

Last on the list is "Friday the 13th"; one of the most famous dead habit.
As Friday and 13 both considered unlucky, cohabit.

The list is endless and so is the reason theory,
People have their own version of dead habits story.

SORRY FIGURE

Is sorry really a mighty word or just a tool to help people get away with their blunders?

Do we really feel the repentance while apologising or is it just a word to show our etiquettes?

People have written songs and stories around this, depicting the value sorry word carries.

We have often heard people saying, "You should have at least apologised"

Apologised in the true sense or to satisfy a person's ego on the receiving end?

Sorry is just not about feeling regretful, it is also about being grieved.

It can be associated with pity or with a tragic or an unfortunate situation.

We are more conscious about "cutting a sorry figure" as we don't want people to look down upon us for anything.

Benjamin Franklin rightly said, "Never, never ruin an apology with an excuse" as then the value becomes nil.

A sorry figure should never be seen with respect to age, status, gender, because a malfeasance is a malfeasance, no matter who committed it.

Sorry might not undo wrongs but it should certainly be used when committing a mistake unintentionally because intentional mistakes do not have a place for a sorry figure!

DESTINY REVEALS THE SECRET

Sam was a very mischievous boy,
His heart was that of a sepoy.
He belonged to a business clan,
His father was not a rich businessman.

Once when scolded by his mother for breaking the
vase,
Gave a bitter retort, "At least I did not bring any
disgrace".
Sam was a student of grade five,
Loved to play with weapons and knife.

A family secret was hidden from him.
He was unaware of his elder brother "Kim",
Who was behind bars,
Had gone from his family too far.

Kim had murdered a woman for want of money.
This news was certainly uncanny.
He was just 15 yeas old when he committed the
crime,
The pain for his parents is unbearable till this time.

Sam on the other hand was cheerful & easy going,
But at times it seemed as if in him, his brother's
seeds were sowing.
He frequently asked from his parents money,
Irrespective of the day being rainy or sunny.

Once when he was refused,
At his parents behaviour he was amused.
From childhood he was very close to his aunt.
He called her immediately to rant.

She mistakenly revealed the secret of Kim to Sam,
Between him and his family she constructed a
hatred dam.
Sam felt bad; for his parents did not tell him
earlier,
He felt cheated and regarded himself a failure.

Sam left his home late at night,
He was unaware of life's dreadful tide.
His want of money made him a smuggler.
His life had become gloomy with no colour.

But suddenly his destiny took a turn.
The turn was a huge concern.
He was thrown into a lockup with a prison mate.
He was certainly not in a good state.

The two talked from dawn until dusk.
The two shared a bond of unbreakable trust.
What a coincidence! Both were released the same
day.
They promised to meet each other in the month of
May.

Sam took a short cut to his sweet home.
He was in a hurry to go far from this tomb.
But Kim took a long road,
He was uncertain whether his house should he
again board.

Sam reached home, his parents were filled with
euphoria.
Celebrations were arranged as if for the queen
Victoria.
Suddenly the door bell rang,
Sam opened the door with a bang.

He was happy to see his partner on the door.
Sam asked, "What are you here for?"
Sam's parents shouted, "Whose there?"
Sam stood aside to let his parents stare.

His parents cried, "Kim you're back!"
The family's happiness shall never find a cul-de-sac.

I WILL DO

What kind of person am I?
It's a mystery which is difficult to untie.

I want my life the way I think.
If it goes astray I might sink.

What I need to understand is to be happy at all times,
Not always our life with our thinking rhymes.

Do my best and leave the rest,
Celebrate every moment like a fest.

I need to count my achievements and my blessings.
And not just me but to all I am addressing.

I know I will make everyone around me proud,
Even if at this point it is difficult to see a silver lining in the cloud.

I have to do & I will do
You'll see all my friends and foe.

SIGNIFICANCE OF GREETINGS

Meets and Greets are an important form of
communication,
If done in the right way, can bring in a lot of
appreciation.

"Namaste" is what we associate with greeting form
in India,
Placing both hands together in a prayer position is
the main idea.

"Bow" is how we greet in Japan,
Facing each other and lowering our upper body, as
we stand.

"Firm handshake", used widely, is Russia's
important form,
Regard and respect is needed, without thinking
much about the norm.

"Touching Nose" is what we associate with New
Zealand,
With greetings spirits will elevate and not weaken.

"Kiss on right cheek" and "Kiss on each cheek",
both are different greetings stance,
One is followed in Argentina and the other in
France.

"Snapping fingers handshake" is prevalent in
Nigeria,
Seems a way to express excitement and euphoria.

"Mano" is a polite way followed widely in
Philippines,
Soft and full of respect it appeals.

Whatever be the way of greeting or showing
respect,
The forms mentioned are just one aspect.

What is important is the unconditional love and
support,
Irrespective of the person's abode.

TURN DREAMS INTO REALITY

Half of our life goes into aspirations, hopes, and
grails,
Oftenly, we get baffled with which one is a success
and which one a fail.

Silently fantasizing is the most sought-after
pastime,
Endeavour is needed to make a soothing chime.

The first step to a fulfilling life is Introspection;
Sort and filter the goals and remove the negation.

The second step is to find the pros and the cons;
Not let it be at the cost of anyone, stress your pons.

Generally, we tend to drop out after the second
step;
And leave our dreams under the web.

Because the third step involves execution;
With lots and lots of permutation and combination.

In the interim what goes futile is the time;
Our visions drop low which were once sublime.

We start giving importance to the by products;
All our fantasies become total bollocks.

What is needed to turn it around is diligence.
To grab the fruit that's just across the fence.

DIGNITY OF LABOUR

Every kind of work has its own significance,
And the one who does it knows its due diligence.

We can become jack of all trades but not master of
all,
A master is certainly needed in the entire journey,
to save us from the fall.

That's when comes the "Dignity of Labour".
Respecting all professions is not a favour.

What goes into every task is only known by the
performers,
No matter how much we try to degrade it with
misnomers.

The love and loyalty one has with the work, which
makes one a bread winner,
Is often neglected by people who disrespect,
thereby becoming a sinner.

The labour can be performed mentally or
physically,
And there is no way one could or should ever tally.

What may be dignified for us may not be for
others,

Thus, every occupation has its own dignity no
matter what one prefers.

Before asking our counterparts to respect what we
do,
Having conviction in ourselves is important with a
clear view.

REVOLUTIONS & LEARNINGS

The **Neolithic Revolution (10,000 BCE - 4,000 BCE)**
marked the transition from hunting and
gathering to settled Agriculture,
Learned development of permanent settlements,
domestication of animals and emergence
of complex societies culture.

The **Industrial Revolution (18th - 19th Centuries) was**
all about mechanised manufacturing processes
and technologies,
It taught humans productivity, urbanisation and the
significance of capitalism ideologies.

1775 - 1783 was the period of
American Revolution,
leading to the formation of a sovereign state :
"United Nations".
The revolution inspired movements for
independence, sovereignty and
democratic relations.

The **French Revolution (1789 - 1799)**
overthrew the absolute monarchy and
feudal system in France,
Taught importance of revolutionary
movements and political upheaval trance.

The only successful slave revolt in history was the
Haitian Revolution (1791 - 1804),
Which was all about the abolition of slavery and
getting independence from the domination.

The **Russian Revolution (1917)** happened in
2 phases which led to the establishment of
the Soviet Union,
The great learnings from this revolution were
the power of the masses, importance of
leadership and communion.

Led by the Communist Party, the **Chinese
Revolution (1949)** resulted in the establishment of
the People's Republic of China.
The revolution taught the determination of
bringing out change and ended centuries old

imperial rule in China.

1979 is remembered as a year of **Iranian Revolution** that led to the establishment of Islamic Republic.
It completely changed the political landscape of middle east to establish rules in favour of the public.

These are some of the revolutions that brought about a significant impact on the world history, The struggle, blood, sweat, change and determination went in to paint it glittery.

POWER OF THE MIND

Consciously or unconsciously our mind is filled with a lot of feelings and emotions.

But how do we know what thoughts belong to our conscious mind & what to our unconscious mind?

It is said, some unacceptable thoughts and those we are unaware of, primarily, are present in our unconscious part.

They are dormant unless or until they are triggered by any emotion closely related to them.

And when our unconscious mind becomes active, we become dormant.

We lose the power of rumination, the power of decision making, the power of distinguishing between right and wrong, and also the power to hold us from going astray.

Then what is the difference between unconscious & subconscious?

Unconscious part happens automatically and it is not within our control but subconscious part can be controlled if we wish to.

There is some cognition which simply gets stored in the brain but we do not bring it to our focal awareness, it comes upfront only when we think about it consciously.
This is what subconscious is.

As clearly visible, our thoughts control our life, be it consciously, subconsciously or unconsciously.

And so, it becomes all the more important to keep a track of our thoughts. Right?

Actions and reactions are a product of our cogitation and thus it is must to be aware of what is fed to our mind!

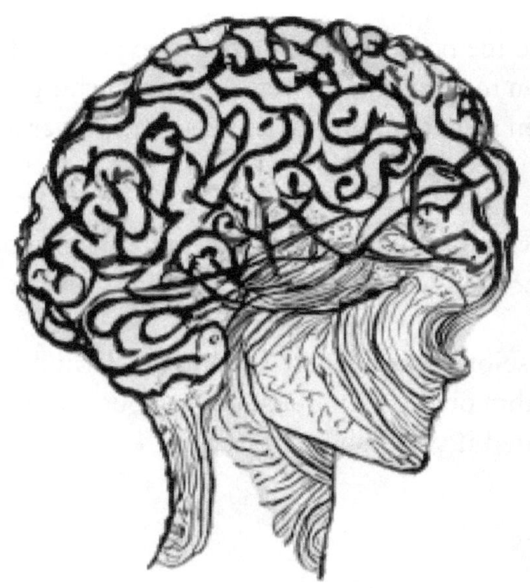

BURDEN OF EXPECTATIONS

Projections are dangerous if done merely by
assuming things beforehand.
They can degrade or upgrade one based on the
level of expectations;
And because of these presumptions one becomes
quite pretentious,
Pretentious to stand up and meet up the
expectations.

In the process one tends to forget the real self and
attempts to conform to the world's expectations,
Expectations not only harm the one who tries to
meet them but also the one who grows them
within;
Because what is already pictured in the mind may
not be replicated.
And thus the adage "Communication is the key."

As without the exchange of thoughts how will the
reality thrive?
Yes, it is good to meet the expectations to elevate
and push oneself for the best,
but not at the cost of losing oneself entirely and
forgetting what one truly loves.
Hence, lower the weight of suppositions and
increase the projection of reality to have a
balanced Beam Of Life!

RELATIVE OR ABSOLUTE

We certainly live relatively in the world; however,
we may deny it,
Since we do not like to be judged in comparison to
our counterparts,
As relative is associated with dependence and
absolute with independence;

But deep inside we all know what we do in life is
relative to what others have done.
It is said food, shelter, clothing are the basic
necessities and that is what we need.
So, what about our wants, aren't they relative?
Aren't the desires relative?

What is the definition of a good life? A definition
based on relative parameters.
The life with which we are unsatisfied maybe is a
desired one elsewhere.
The life we desire maybe is the most undesired life
for the one who is experiencing it.

All this is relative and that is what makes all the
difference.
It is good to be relative as it pushes us to do
something better each day.
as long as it doesn't come at a cost. A major cost
resulting in repentance.

Relativeness is multiplicative, if righteous, can
help in flourishing else if unjustifiable, will surely
lead us to perish.
Absoluteness on the other hand is additive, it only
adds value to one's life with respect to oneself.

BEING COURTEOUS

Portraying our good form will not have negative
consequences,
But will surely enlighten the mood of the
counterpart.

If we have nothing to lose, why not contribute to
somebody's gain?
We may not know when we might trigger
someone's Achilles heel.
Though inadvertently, that trigger may leave a
mark on else's mind.

Not to confuse portraying good form, with
pleasing others;
Just a modest gesture in any form might help,
however minute it may be.

Courtesy is a kind of investment where we
shouldn't expect any return.
The returns we get could be in various forms from
"Goodwill" to a "Great bond" to "Blessings" to
"An aid when we require" or simply a humane
gesture purifying our soul.

PROFESSIONS

Professions span over a wide range of fields and
industries,
Each serving specific functions with different
boundaries.
Let's classify them into 12 broad categories,
And understand each profession through
allegories.

Healthcare includes doctors, nurse, surgeon,
pharmacist, dentists,
And all medical researchers, physical and
occupational therapists.
Necessary for promoting health, treating illness
and improving quality of life,
Preventing spread of diseases and supporting good
lifestyle.

Protection of rights, liberties and maintenance of
law and stability,
Resolving disputes and ensuring justice and
fairness in society;
Is looked after by lawyer, judge, paralegal, legal
secretary, legal consultant and aid worker,
Together constituting legal profession; responsible
for regulation of behaviour.

Empowering individuals, enriching communities,
and advancing society's progress,
Is associated with education profession, nurturing
the next generation's newness.
Teacher, Professor, School Administrator,
Guidance Counselor, Librarian, Educational
Psychologist, all contribute to this foundational
and integral profession,
Helping individuals discover talents, pursue
aspirations and have a great progression.

CEO, Manager, Accountant, Human Resources
Specialist, Marketing Specialist, Financial Analyst
and Operations Managers,
All fall under one profession; Business and
Management; having their own set of parameters.
Guiding organisations towards their goals,
ensuring sustainability and contributing to
economic well being,
The scope enhances to implementing controls,
safeguarding, mitigating risks and contingency
plans foreseeing.

IT professions are in demand they say,
For them, there is no difference between night and
day.
Software/Web Developer, Network/Database
Administrator and Systems/Cybersecurity
Analysts,
Are said to be one of the career catalysts.

They mainly involve the use of technology to
manage and process information.
Design, develop, maintain softwares and
applications to build a tech nation.

One of parent's favourite profession is
Engineering,
Civil, Mechanical, Electrical, Chemical,
Aerospace, Environmental, Software are this
profession's steering.
Infrastructure development, manufacturing,
production, electronics, telecommunication,
aerospace, defence, environmental protection,
quality assurance and process optimisation,
Require a lot of training, commitment, a great
education and lots of hands on experience to excel
in this profession.

Artist, Graphic Designer, Writer, Photographer,
Musician, Filmmaker, Actor,
Are a few creative professions and especially right
brain's factor,
Encompassing a wide range of roles that involve
artistic expression, innovation, and problem-
solving,
From designing, animating, managing, directing,
photography, 3D modelling & acting.

Public & Government Services are said to be one
of the most sort out professions,
Politician, Civil Servant, Diplomat, Social Worker,
Police Officer, Firefighter or Emergency Medical
Technician are its priced possessions,
From serving the public interest, to implementing
government policies to managing resources, to
upholding democratic principles, and ensuring
effective government decisions,
Not all can make way in their life for such
obsessions.

Science & Research professions require a great
deal of knowledge and passion,
Be it scientist, researcher, biologist, chemist,
physicist, astronomer or geologist faction.
Exploring, understanding, expanding knowledge,
driving innovation and addressing challenge,
Along with dealing with changing environmental
phenomenas and striking a balance.

Skilled Trades Professions have their own special
place in the list,
Without carpenter, electrician, plumber, welder,
mechanic, mason it would be difficult to exist.
Contributing to construction, manufacturing,
infrastructure, and maintenance projects that
support communities and economies,
They require specialized training, hands-on
experience and technical expertise.

Becoming a voice to the masses is noble and
crucial,
Media and communications profession deal with
these socials.
Journalist, Public Relations Specialist, Editor,
Broadcast News Analyst, Social Media Manager,
Content Creator and Copywriter are the various
types,
Creating, disseminating, managing information
and content along with exposing oneself to mass
likes and dislikes.

At the end on the list is Hospitality and Tourism
Profession,
Catering to the needs and experiences of travellers,
guests, and visitors with gentle expression.
Hotel manager, chef, event planner, tour guide,
travel agent, Sommelier and Concierge are a few
diverse examples,
Each role plays a crucial part in creating enjoyable
and memorable experience samples.

NAVIGATING LIFE SITUATIONS

Encountering one of the biggest fears of life is apparently astonishing.
The one who actually witnesses it, knows the hunch.

Contemplating things before their occurrence will only shatter one.
Either the event doesn't happen or it happens on a scale beyond one's imagination.

Then lost is the time when smooth and calm were the waves and lost is the time when tides took place.
Eventually left behind are the shadowed days, shadowed with gloom and despair.

Preparation for the worst? Of course, is ideal.
Ruminating on it for long? Of course, isn't.

Dreading on the missing forethought of any unprecedented situation in place turns the scenario pitch dark.
What is needed is the pragmatic submission of whatever one has to offer to flatten the agony.

But when it is right before one's sight, the mind overlooks its vision.
Doors are closed! not a single ray of hope! is what one feels.

The one who rises from the downfall & misery has stories to tell of the healing power of time and recreation of the scenery.

JUDGEMENTAL

We all have a multi-faceted personality,
Trying to figure out which facet to open and when.

The one who masters the skill becomes a people's
person,
But the one who struggles at this is looked down
upon.

And from here starts the categorisation of people
based on our perception.
But wait, does it end here?

This is just the beginning of we becoming victims
of unconscious bias,
Trying to see through people with the eyes of
others and moulding our thoughts based on the
experiences of others.

And then we tend to give birth to negative vibes
for people we don't even know.
As per version of Eleanor Roosevelt, "Learn from
the mistakes of others, you cannot live long
enough to make them yourself". So apt and true.
Right?

But hold on, does it apply everywhere? Are we
capable enough to differentiate when to apply and
when to not?

There is also this problem of being candid.
For a person who is blunt and above board, the
world tries to make fun and enjoy.

All this collectively leads us to become
"JUDGEMENTAL"!

REMINDER

Have we started living with the life problems or
have we not?
Have we overcome our inner fears and fought?
Are we still just sitting back and prattling?
Or are we coming upfront and battling?
In what way are we taking a stance?
Will it happen on its own perchance?
Are we taking a rain check on the situation?
Are we showing some concern and consideration?
Don't you think it is easier said than done?
Can't we just turn the tables, get this phase
undone?
Only the sufferers know the real worry,
Are we here to just feel sorry?
It's easier to teach than preach,
Surely this piece is not just for speech.
This is to remind me too,
Of all the services I am obliged to!

GREY ADULTING QUESTIONS

What is ADULTING?

Is it associated merely with a particular age number?
Is it associated with the way we act?
Is it associated with the activities we perform?
Or is it associated with the way we communicate?

When shall we draw a line between childhood and adulthood?
Does society judge us more when we reach the adulthood stage?
Are we really fully independent to take our own decisions?
And does adulting make us lose our innocence?

Do we become more conscious of what "others" think of us?
Are we strong enough to accept the way we are or do we change ourselves to please others?
Do we have the audacity to put our point across firmly and clearly?
Do we readily accept what is fed to our ears and eyes or do we question and find out a reason?

Are the responsibilities during adulthood forced on us?
Is adulting experienced only when we move out of our comfort zones?
Are we ready to understand and answer all the above 15 questions?

IF YES, CONGRATULATIONS WE ARE INTO ADULTHOOD LEGITIMATELY!

A NOTE TO SELF!

Make your approach towards goals flexible and be open to amendments,

Leave aside your vulnerability and antiquate it with resiliency,

The messiness is what adds a grain of salt to your perception,

Blessed are the flexible, for they shall not be bent out of shape because of the change,

Your stance at the unprecedented time is what defines your persona,

I learned it years ago but realized now!

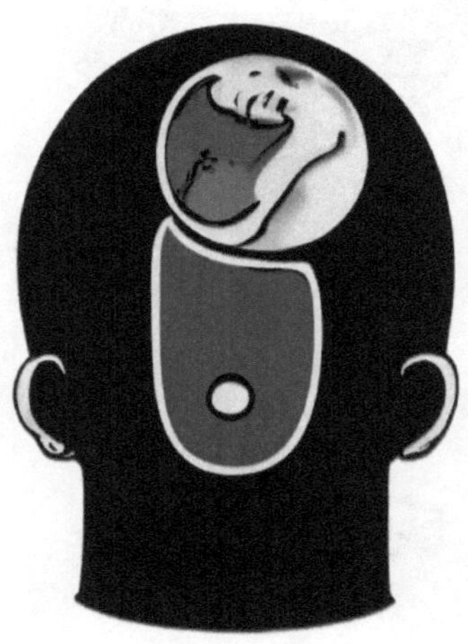

NATURE'S WISDOM

From being Static to being Dynamic,
From Gaucheness to Savoir Faire,
From Baffled to Clear,
From Ashes to Phoenix,
From Achilles Heel to Forte,
From Gloom to Flamboyance,
From Dull to Vivacious,
From Many to One & Only,
The versions belong to nature solely,
Let's not spoil and nurture it wholly.

SOCIAL STRATIFICATION

Grouping and characterization is seen everywhere,
Be it in a society we live in, a school, an office or
any kind of institution.
Though the ways and factors may differ according
to the backdrop.

This is what leads to Social Stratification,
Where the different strata or layers signify the
cluster.
It even takes the form of ranking based on wealth,
income, race, education and power.
It can even turn a life sweet and can also turn it
sour.

For some, status is inherited while for others it is
earned.
The vertical movement of strata is what makes it
even worse,
The unequal ways of arrangement can give birth to
hatred and judgement,
Even if there is difference with respect to socio
economic indicators.

What is needed is equal stance and opportunity for
one and all.
As it is easy to say "It's all because of Destiny"
But difficult to realize, it is we who design it.

We have the power to define our own individuality,
to place ourselves in a group, or to let others do it
for us. The choice is ours. Decide!

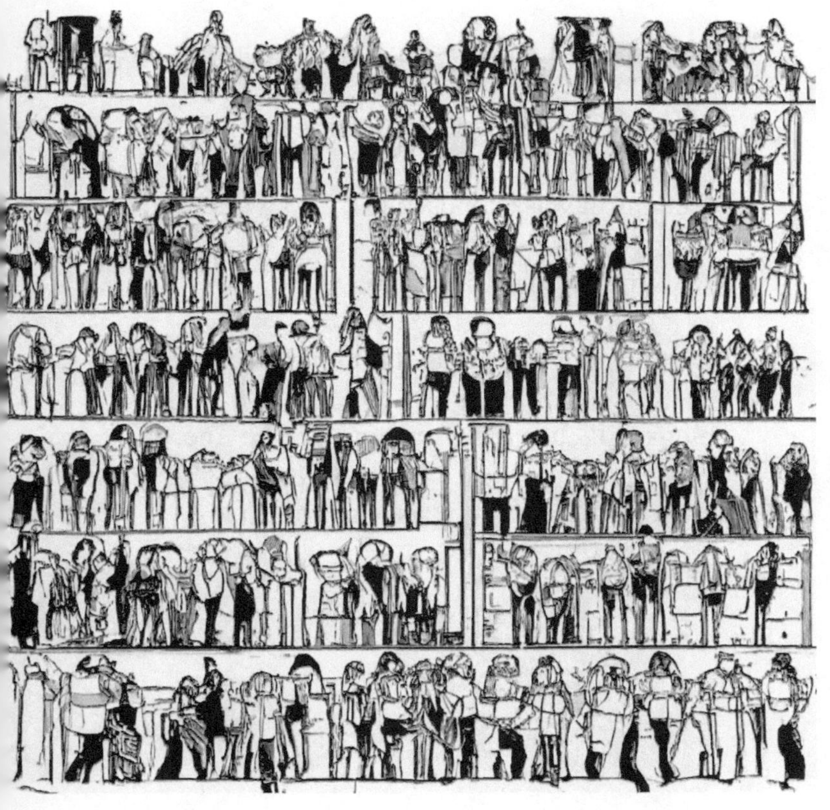

ROSY PICTURE

For me as a post millennial;

The thought of adulting was quite surreal,

Was coping with the rules of the world,

Didn't know challenges would put on a spurt.

I was just sympathizing with myself;

When mirth was supposed to overpower wealth.

How can I be so selfish and insane,

When the world is going through misery and pain.

Things will change; everything will be fine,

All we can do right now is just unite.

UNSAID ECHOES

I wonder why are we interested in what other's wear, what other's eat and in what kind of shelter other's live?

STAND UP!! SPEAK UP!! FIGHT FOR YOUR RIGHTS!! very commonly heard but why does the one who practices it is left aloof even by his/her near and dear ones?

PEOPLE SHOULD NOT BE ASHAMED OF MENTAL ISSUES!! So when the person tries to express his mental instability why does he/she become a topic of discussion/entertainment? Do we really forget the past and the achievements of that person when he/she was completely sound?

Why do we take favours and then TURN A DEAF EAR when the same person who helped us is in dire need?

Why does fear of missing out/jealousy creep inside us? Why don't we have a life of our own? Why don't we realize that the person we are jealous of has put in a lot of sweat and blood to be where he/she is and is his/her destiny?

Why are we always ready to point out fingers at others? It is really easy to play a blame game. Before blaming we should question ourselves what would we have done if we were in their place.

We shall question ourselves what have we done for our parents? What have we given to them? Do we have a plan of giving them in double and lessen up their burden in all ways?

It is important to love our family as much as possible. Life is too short to twine ourselves into misunderstandings and spoil the relationships. Try to understand the intention of the person. Be open to suggestions and try to have healthy discussions without age bar.

Everyone has a circular life. What we send out comes back to us. The choice is ours what to send. If someone is going through hardships be empathetic as we may trod on the same path at some point.

It is easy to judge a person in their tough times. But before judging we should question ourselves are we even at par with that person? Have we done much in life to be able to judge someone? If yes, let your actions speak not mere words.

JUST PONDER!!PONDER!! PONDER!!